The Mother Deer

The Mother Deer

by Edith Thacher Hurd

Illustrated by Clement Hurd

Boston   **Little, Brown and Company**   Toronto

LIBRARY OF CONGRESS CATALOG CARD NO. 74-182248

Second Printing

Library of Congress Cataloging in Publication Data

Hurd, Edith (Thacher) 1910-
    The mother deer.

    SUMMARY: Describes a year in the life of a mother deer from the birth of her fawns to her mating again and the birth of another set of fawns.
    1. Deer--Juvenile literature. [1. White-tailed deer. 2. Deer] I. Hurd, Clement, 1908-   illus. II. Title.
QL737.U55H87   599'.7357   74-182248
ISBN 0-316-38322-8

Published simultaneously in Canada
by Little, Brown & Company (Canada) Limited

PRINTED IN THE UNITED STATES OF AMERICA

The mother white-tailed deer walked slowly through the meadow toward the pond. Her big ears twitched back and forth. She held her head high and sniffed the fresh spring wind. But there was no danger.

The mother deer was very careful now because she could not run fast. The little fawns that had been growing inside her for six months, would soon be born.

She drank the cold water of the pond and ate the fresh grass of the meadow. When she had finished, she went back into the woods and lay quietly under the tall trees.

Just as the sun went down, and the night was beginning to come, the little fawns were born. Their reddish-brown coats were covered with white spots. Their big ears were still pressed close to their heads. Their tiny hoofs were soft so that they would not hurt the mother deer.

Almost as soon as they were born, the little fawns tried to stand up. They were hungry and wanted to reach their mother. But their long legs were not strong enough to hold them. When the mother deer licked them clean with her rough tongue, the babies toppled over and fell to the ground.

The mother deer lay down beside them and the fawns nursed her. They drank the warm milk as they lay safe and quiet beside their mother. When they could not drink any more, the little fawns curled up close to each other and slept.

The mother deer left them and went to drink at
the pond and graze in the meadow. The moon
came up and shone on the pond, where two raccoons wet their paws and a mother fox drank
quickly—for she too had new babies to care for.

The baby deer were quite safe in the woods. When the bright sun shone through the trees in the early morning, the white spots on the fawns' reddish-brown coats looked like white sunshine on the brown leaves. The little deer were like a part of the forest.

No hungry animal passing through the woods could smell the new fawns, for while they were so young they had no smell.

When the mother deer came back into the deep woods, the little fawns were awake and strong enough to stand on their thin legs. They came close to their mother and drank her warm milk. They were hungry after sleeping for so long.

When they had finished, the mother deer moved
away from them. She did not look like a part of
of the forest and she had the strong smell of a
deer. It would be easy for another animal to
find her.

The fawns tried to follow their mother as she stepped quietly through the dry leaves. But the mother would not let them. She butted with her head and pushed at the fawns until they lay down again and curled up beside each other.

The mother never went very far from her babies
or stayed away very long. Sometimes she fed
them as many as ten times each day and the little
fawns grew strong.

But still the mother deer would not let the two babies follow her, no matter how hard they tried. Sometimes she raised one of her front legs with its strong, hard hoof, and pushed at the fawns, forcing them to lie down again.

Day after day passed. For three weeks the little fawns lay hidden in the woods. Their legs grew strong. Their hoofs turned hard and sharp and ready for running. Now the mother deer did not stop them from following her to the pond. The fawns drank with the fox and her babies.

Spring turned to summer. The little fawns went to the pond every evening and played in the meadow in the moonlight of the summer nights. Sometimes they butted each other, or they butted at their mother. Sometimes they leaped high in the air, playing leapfrog over each other.

During the long hot days of the summer, the fawns slept in the woods or chased yellow butterflies or crackling crickets humming in the forest.

One day, when a blue jay screamed from the top of a tree, and two crows flew cawing over the meadow, the little deer ran to find out what was happening.

A great eagle flew low over the meadow.

The mother deer led her babies quickly into a deep thicket of pine trees. They stood without moving for a long time. The young deer listened, with their ears pointing forward and then back. Their sharp eyes watched the sky for the eagle. Their heads held high, they sniffed for a smell of danger.

Summer passed. The woods looked as if they were on fire, with red and golden leaves. The birds, like black shadows over the sky, flew south for the winter. The chipmunk filled a hole in an old oak tree, storing it with nuts and seeds for the snowy months ahead.

Wild apples hung from the trees. The mother took whole apples and crunched them in her mouth. The fawns nibbled on the low-hanging apples. They did not drink milk from their mother anymore. The days grew colder. The fawns lost their white spots as their coats turned to gray.

The mother deer grew crinkly gray fur that would keep her warm through cold winter nights. But before the winter began, a big buck, a father deer, came to run through the woods with the doe.

Sometimes another buck also came to be near the mother deer. Then the big buck lowered his head and stamped his great hooves. Sometimes the two bucks fought, crashing their strong antlers together.

When the buck and the doe ran through the woods together, the fawns could hardly keep up with them. But the mother deer used her white tail as a signal. Flashing it up and down, she showed the fawns which way she had gone and guided them through the dark woods.

The north wind blew harder each day. It danced the yellow and red leaves in the air and blew the brown acorns from the oak trees. The big buck and the doe and the fawns fed on the acorns. They grew fat and sleek, and ready for the hungry days of the winter.

One night when the stars shone as bright as the eyes of the mother fox and her young, and as bright as the eyes of the raccoons at the pond, and the eyes of the chipmunk in the old tree, the buck and the doe mated. Just as she had done the autumn before and the autumn before that, the doe mated with a big buck.

Winter came and snow fell softly until the ground was covered with fresh white snow. The big buck went away, into a faraway part of the woods, and there he lost his spreading antlers because he did not need them anymore. But new horns would grow again, soft as velvet in the spring but strong and sharp when it was time for him to fight for a doe in the fall.

The young deer stayed with their mother all winter. They slept near her in the snow and ate the dry grass under the snow. But at last the snow was too deep in the woods and even down in the meadow. The deer stretched their necks to reach the small branches of the trees and they chewed at the bark, but as the winter went on, they were often hungry.

At last the warm sun shone again. The snow melted. The meadow began to turn green. Now the mother deer would not let the young deer stay with her anymore. She butted and pushed at them until they went off into the woods together.

The mother deer wandered by herself. Then she lay down in the thick bushes. The spring sun warmed her, and she gave birth to her two new little fawns, just as she had done the spring before and the spring before that.